READING RESPONSE FORMS

Literacy Skills Series

Written by Eleanor M. Summers

GRADES 1 – 2

Classroom Complete Press
P.O. Box 19729
San Diego, CA 92159
Tel: 1-800-663-3609 | Fax: 1-800-663-3608
Email: service@classroomcompletepress.com

www.classroomcompletepress.com

ISBN-13: 978-1-55319-398-2
ISBN-10: 1-55319-398-9

Critical Thinking Skills

Reading Response Forms Grades 1-2

Level	Skills For Critical Thinking	Word Study	Comprehension	Reading Response	Writing Tasks	Graphic Organizers
LEVEL 1 Remembering	• Understands Word Meanings And Text	✓				✓
	• Identifies Parts Of Speech: Nouns, Verbs, Adjectives	✓				✓
	• Recall Details	✓	✓	✓	✓	✓
	• Identify Story Sections: Beginning, Middle, End	✓	✓	✓	✓	✓
LEVEL 2 Understanding	• Character Study		✓	✓	✓	✓
	• Sequence And Summarize Events		✓			
	• Identify The Main Idea		✓	✓		
	• Describe Characters, Setting	✓	✓		✓	✓
	• Interpret Ideas		✓	✓	✓	
LEVEL 3 Applying	• Select And State Information	✓	✓			✓
	• Identify The Outcome			✓		
	• Apply New Learning			✓	✓	
	• Make Connections To Personal Experiences And To Real Life		✓	✓	✓	
LEVEL 4 Analysing	• Draw Conclusions		✓	✓	✓	
	• Find Proof In The Story	✓	✓	✓		
	• Infer Character Motivation			✓	✓	
	• Identify Cause And Effect	✓		✓		✓
	• Make Inferences Using Personal Experiences			✓	✓	
LEVEL 5 Evaluating	• Develop And Express An Opinion			✓	✓	✓
	• Make Judgments			✓	✓	
	• Ask Questions				✓	
LEVEL 6 Creating	• Make Predictions			✓	✓	
	• Give Personal Interpretation Of Story			✓	✓	
	• Create				✓	
	• Imagine Alternatives To Story			✓	✓	

Based on Bloom's Taxonomy

Contents

TEACHER GUIDE

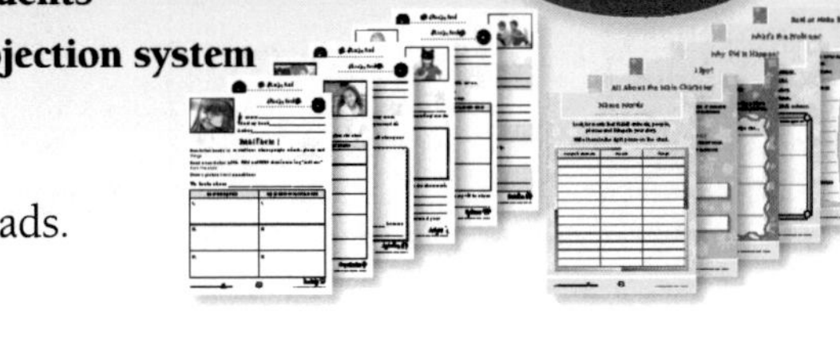

Assessment Rubric

Reading Response Forms Grades 1-2

Student's Name: ______________ Assignment: ______________ Level: ________

	Level 1	Level 2	Level 3	Level 4
Comprehension of Story Content	• Demonstrates a limited understanding of story content • Requires teacher intervention	• Demonstrates a basic understanding of story content • Requires some teacher intervention	• Demonstrates a good understanding of story content • Requires minimal teacher intervention	• Demonstrates a thorough understanding of story content • Requires no teacher intervention
Response to the Text	• Expresses responses to the text with limited effectiveness	• Expresses responses to the text with some effectiveness	• Expresses responses to the text with appropriate skills	• Expresses thorough and complete responses to the text
Analysis and Application of Key Concepts	• Interprets and applies various concepts in the text with few unrelated details	• Interprets and applies various concepts in the text with some details	• Interprets and applies various concepts in the text with appropriate details	• Effectively interprets and applies various concepts in the text with consistent, clear and effective details

STRENGTHS:

WEAKNESSES:

NEXT STEPS:

Teacher Guide

Our resource has been created for ease of use by both TEACHERS and STUDENTS alike.

Introduction

Our Reading Response Forms allow the young readers to share their thinking about the literature they have heard or read themselves. Reading response also gives readers the opportunity to demonstrate their understanding of the materials. Responses can range from personal, which relates to present and past experiences and knowledge, to new learning. The variety of responses can be oral, written, dramatic, musical or visual.

- Students can complete activities on their own, freeing the teacher to work with small groups or conference individual readers.
- Reading response provides for student choice and values individual opinions and experiences. They encourage connections between literature and real life.

Also provided are four Hands-On Activities, a word search and a crossword. The Assessment Rubric (page 4) is a useful tool for evaluating students' responses to many of the activities in our resource. The Comprehension Quiz (page 53) can be used for either a follow-up review or assessment at the completion of the unit.

How Is Our Resource Organized?

STUDENT HANDOUTS - READING RESPONSE FORMS

- Teachers can use response forms to extend your student's reading experience by offering a wide variety of activities. Early readers need to explore literature and recognize that stories are a beginning point for expanding their ideas and language.
- Teachers can use our forms to assess student understanding and connections to previous learning.
- The reader builds meaning from the text and applies any prior related knowledge.
- The reader explores conventions and ideas about written materials. Reading response provides a reason to closely examine and reread written materials.

PICTURE CUES

Our resource contains three main types of pages, each with a different purpose and use. A **Picture Cue** at the top of each page shows, at a glance, what the page is for.

Teacher Guide
- Information and tools for the teacher

Student Handout
- Reproducible worksheets and activities

The Critical Thinking Skill **Picture Cues** are located at the bottom right of each work sheet.

Teacher Guide

GETTING READY TO BEGIN:

- Provide a wide selection of reading materials to accommodate reading levels and interest.
- Keep folders of various **Reading Response Forms** available for student selection.
- Model and demonstrate each form in a mini-lesson.
- Share and discuss examples of completed forms from previous classes.
- Make a **Reading Response Form** Folder for each child.
- Develop a schedule for individual conferences and group activities.
- Encourage students to select a variety of response forms.

MINI-LESSON FORMAT

- Select a book for shared reading that reflects the skill focus of the **Reading Response Form**.
- Use the supplied **Overhead Transparencies** to facilitate student understanding (or download the Overheads from our web site if you are using a computer projection system. See page 3 for download instructions).
- Use a "Think and Talk Aloud" strategy as you model how to complete the form. Encourage student discussion and responses.
- Use the mini-lesson to introduce and practice new **Reading Response Forms**.
- After teaching and modeling several forms, students may proceed to work independently.

Reading response may take the form of:

Whole class response: Establish a whole class routine so that the students understand how to respond and what to respond to. Displaying the routine plan on a chart may be helpful.

Small group response: Use guided reading groups or literature circles for response opportunities.

Individual responses: Provide a class sharing time for individual response. Allow for enough time for students to proudly present their achievements. Display student work for other classes to see. Consider visiting other classes to share responses or sharing with reading buddies.

HELPING STUDENTS CHOOSE APPROPRIATE BOOKS:

- **Shared Reading:** Teacher is reading text aloud to class. Text can be at any reading level. This is a great opportunity to select based on student interest, unusual topics, science or social studies related topics.
- **Guided Reading**: Students within the group should be able to read with 90 - 95% accuracy rate. This text may be somewhat harder than at the independent level. Teacher will provide assistance as required.
- **Independent Reading:** Help students to understand the "just right" concept. Books should be chosen at this level. The student should be able to read any page with not more than five reading mistakes. Some categories include:
  - Leveled books
  - Easy Readers
  - Joke and Riddle books
  - Chapter books
  - Poetry books
  - Picture books
  - How To books
  - Non-fiction

RUBRICS AND ASSESSMENT (PAGE 4 AND 53):

A rubric is an effective assessment tool for students and teachers. It provides a scoring scale which shows a set of performance criteria and descriptions of achievement of what a reading performance should look like at each point along the leveled continuum. By its format, a rubric can be used as a guide to assessing student performance.

STUDENT SELF-ASSESSMENT RUBRIC (PAGE 8):

- Need to be explained fully to students and modeled for optimum effectiveness.
- Assist students to evaluate their own thinking and personal learning.
- Help students to think about their own performance and consider ways to improve and set goals for future performance.

Individual Student Reading Log

______________'s Reading Log

Date	Title	Author	Number of Pages	Fiction	Non-Fiction

Student Self-Assessment Rubric

Reading Response Forms Grades 1-2

My Name : ________________________________ Grade: ______

Put an **X** in the box that tells about you.

My Thinking

- ☐ I try to be a good listener.
- ☐ I ask for help when I need it.
- ☐ I connect my ideas to the real world.
- ☐ I know the tasks that I do well.
- ☐ I know what I need to try harder on.

My Actions

- ☐ I picked a book that was just right for me.
- ☐ I was organized and ready to work.
- ☐ My work was neatly done and colored.
- ☐ I checked my work for mistakes.
- ☐ I stayed working at my task.

Write a complete answer for each question.

1. What did you enjoy learning the most? Why?

____

____

2. What do you think you need to improve upon in your next task? Why?

____

Bloom's Taxonomy* for Reading Comprehension

The activities in this resource engage and build the full range of thinking skills that are essential for students' reading comprehension. Based on the six levels of thinking in Bloom's Taxonomy, questions are given that challenge students to not only recall what they have read, but move beyond this to understand the text through higher-order thinking. By using higher-order skills of applying, analysing, evaluating and creating, students become active readers, drawing more meaning from the text, and applying and extending their learning in more sophisticated ways.

Our **Reading Response Forms**, therefore, are an effective tool for any Language Arts program. Whether it is used in whole or in part, or adapted to meet individual student needs, this resource provides teachers with the important questions to ask, inspiring students' interest, creativity, and promoting meaningful learning.

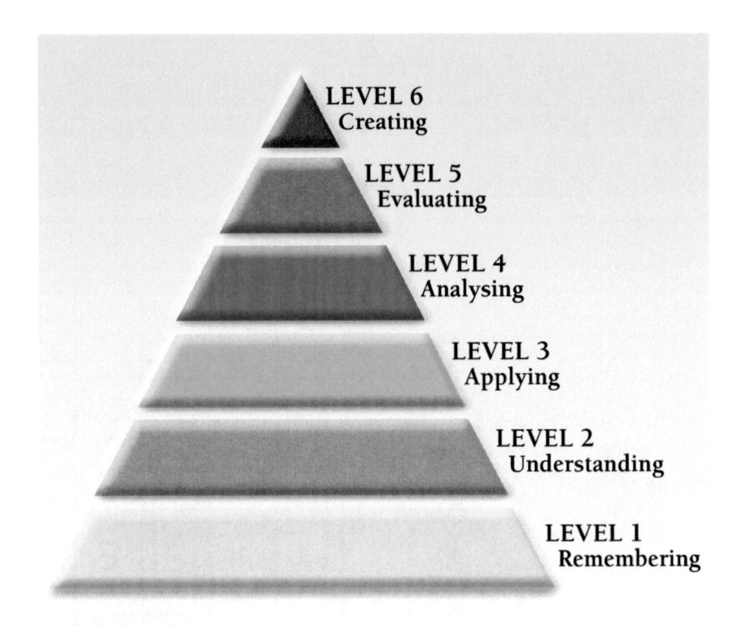

**BLOOM'S TAXONOMY:
6 LEVELS OF THINKING**

****Bloom's Taxonomy is a widely used tool by educators for classifying learning objectives, and is based on the work of Benjamin Bloom.***

Vocabulary

ACTION WORDS

• bark • beg • beep • bounce • bubble • clap • climb • cry • eat • grow • help • hide • hunt • invite • jump • knock • listen • look • play • ride • run • sit • sleep • smile

CHARACTER WORDS

• ant • astronaut • baby • bear • bee • bird • boy • brother • chipmunk • colt • cousin • cub • dad • deer • dog • duck • fish • fox • girl • hen • ladybug • mom • pig • wolf

STORY WORDS

• action • author • beginning • cause • characters • effect • end • ending • idea • main • middle • pictures • problem • rebus • setting • story map • summary • title

Across:

1. eat
2. ride
3. cry
4. sleep
5. jump
6. grow

Down:

1. play
2. run
3. hide
4. smile
5. help
6. sit

51

Word Search Answers

d	o	i	d	a	g	t	n	p	i	g	o
q	b	i	r	d	r	t	d	e	d	i	u
w	e	r	v	o	t	p	b	e	a	r	o
z	x	c	i	g	b	n	o	m	a	l	d
e	m	s	p	d	f	d	y	h	j	r	e
w	o	l	f	v	b	v	b	n	m	n	d
a	m	o	r	d	u	c	k	k	f	d	a
c	l	k	r	a	a	g	y	c	i	b	s
i	q	a	w	d	e	t	x	t	s	y	u
l	t	a	x	d	f	g	r	h	h	e	n

52

EZ✓

1. b)
2. c)
3. c)
4. c)
5. c)
6. c)
7. d)

54

My name: ______________________

Title of my book: ______________________

Author: ______________________

Name Words

Look for words that **name** animals, people, places and things in your story. Write them in the right place on the chart.

People & Animals	Places	Things

Remembering

My name: ______________________________

Title of my book: ______________________

Author: _______________________________

Name Words in Pictures

Name words tell us about **animals, people, places and things**.

Pick **one picture** in your story. Look at it carefully.

Write words that name the **animals, people, places** and **things** you see in the picture.

In the **last box, draw a picture** for **one** of the words in each column.

People & Animals	Places	Things

Remembering

My name: ______________________

Title of my book: ______________________

Author: ______________________

Action Words

Action words tell us what the person, animal or thing is **doing**.

eg. **talking, smiling, looking**

Write 6 good action words from your story.

1. ______________________
2. ______________________
3. ______________________
4. ______________________
5. ______________________
6. ______________________

Draw and **color** a **picture** to show one of your **action words**.

Write the action word under your picture.

Remembering

My name: ______________________________

Title of my book: ______________________________

Author: ______________________________

Interesting Words

Interesting words make a story sound better.

e.g. **terrific, howl, adventure**

Look in your story for **interesting** words.

Write a list of **10 interesting words**.

1. ______________________
2. ______________________
3. ______________________
4. ______________________
5. ______________________
6. ______________________
7. ______________________
8. ______________________
9. ______________________
10. ______________________

Write good sentences for **two** of the words in your list.

1. ____
2. ____

Remembering

My name: ____________________

Title of my book: ____________________

Author: ____________________

Story Summary

A story has three parts: **beginning, middle, end.**

Write what happened in each part of your story.

Draw and **color** a picture to show your answer.

	My Sentences	My Pictures
Beginning		
Middle		
End		

Remembering

After You Read

My name: ____________________

Title of my book: ____________________

Author: ____________________

Do I love you ?
Do [fish] swim ?
Does a [hen] lay [eggs] ?
Is the sky blue ?

Rebus Title

A **rebus** uses pictures for some of the important words like **name words** and **action words**.

Write the **title** of your story:

____

Circle the words that you could draw a picture of.

Now make your **rebus title** using pictures and words.

Share your **rebus title** with a friend to see if they can read your pictures and words.

After You Read

My name: ______________________

Title of my book: ______________________

Author: ______________________

Favorite Character

A **character** is the **person** or **animal** in the story.

Write the name of your favorite character in this story.

____

Why did you pick this character?

____

Draw and **color** a picture to show how your **favorite character** looked in one part of the story.

Remembering

After You Read

My name: ______________________

Title of my book: ______________________

Author: ______________________

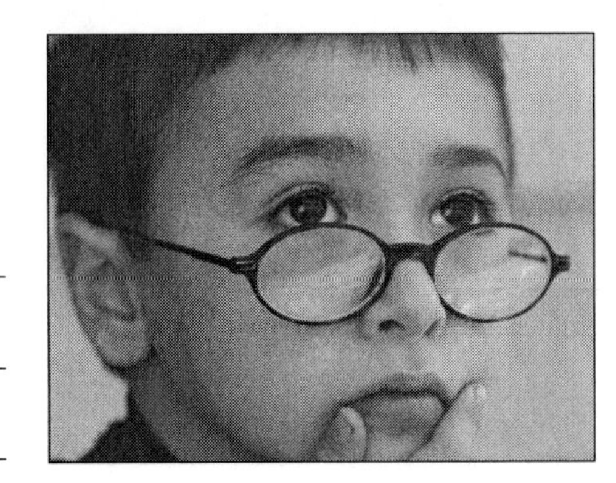

All About the Main Character

The **main character** is the **most important** person or animal in your story.

Think about words that **describe** your character:

- how he or she **looks**
- how he or she **acts** or **behaves**
- how he or she **feels**
- how he or she **treats other characters**

In the box **draw** and **color** a picture to show how your character looks.

On each line, write a word that **describes** your character.

Remembering

My name: ____________________

Title of my book: ____________________

Author: ____________________

Put It All Together!

A **summary** tells **what happened** in the story.

Retell your story in the **order** it happened.

First: ____________________

____

Next: ____________________

____

After that: ____________________

____

Then: ____________________

____

Next: ____________________

____

At the end of the story: ____________________

____

My name: ______________________________

Title of my book: ______________________________

Author: ______________________________

The Main Idea

The **main idea** is what the story is **about**.

What is the **main idea** of your story?

____

What happened in this story? Write **six** of the **main events** in the order that they happened.

1. ______________________________
2. ______________________________
3. ______________________________
4. ______________________________
5. ______________________________
6. ______________________________

What is the most important event in this story? Why?

____

____

Understanding

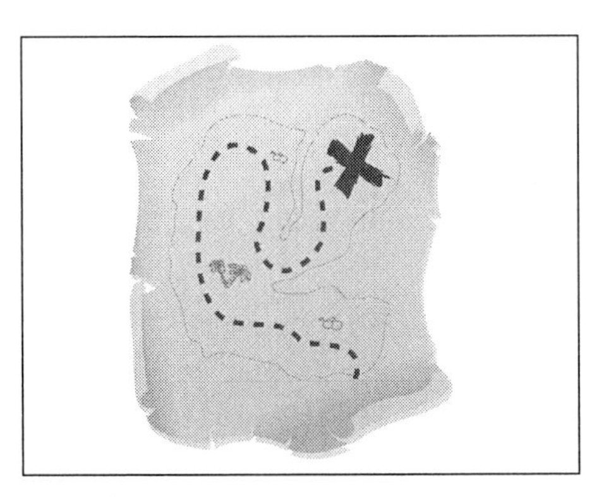

My name: ______________________________

Title of my book: ______________________________

Author: ______________________________

Map of the Setting

The **setting** tells us **where** and **when** the story happens.

Draw and **color** a map to show the setting of your story.

The **setting** is ______________________________

Label your map to show the places in the story.

My Story Map

My name: ______________________

Title of my book: ______________________

Author: ______________________

Sum It Up!

Sum up your story by filling in the chart.

Who? Characters: the people or animals	
Where? Setting:	
When? Setting:	
What happens? Plot:	
Why did this happen?	
Conclusion: How does the story end?	

My name: ____________________

Title of my book: ____________________

Author: ____________________

I Spy!

Good pictures help to tell the story. Pick **two** pictures in your story.

Fill in the chart to tell **what you see** and how the picture **helps to tell** the story.

Then write a **title** for each picture.

I see	The picture helps me ......
1.	
A good title for this picture is:	

2.	
A good title for this picture is:	

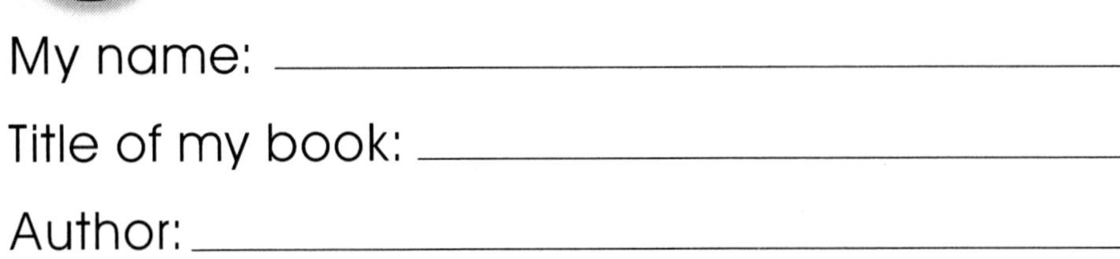

My name: ______________________

Title of my book: ______________________

Author: ______________________

And Then ...

What happened at the very **end** of your story?

____

____

Complete the sentences in your **own words**.

1. I was surprised when ______________________

____

2. I wonder why ______________________

____

3. My favorite part was ______________________

____

4. After this I think ______________________

____

5. Maybe the main character should have ______________________

____

After You Read

My name: ______________________

Title of my book: ______________________

Author: ______________________

You are There!

Pretend that you are the **main character** in your story.

Think about how you would act.

What would you do **differently**? What would you do the **same**?

Complete the chart.

Things I would do differently	Things I would do the same
1.	1.
2.	2.

Draw and **color** a picture to show something that you are doing.

Circle the answer at the bottom of the page.

I am acting the **same as** / **different from** my main character.

My name: ____________________

Title of my book: ____________________

Author: ____________________

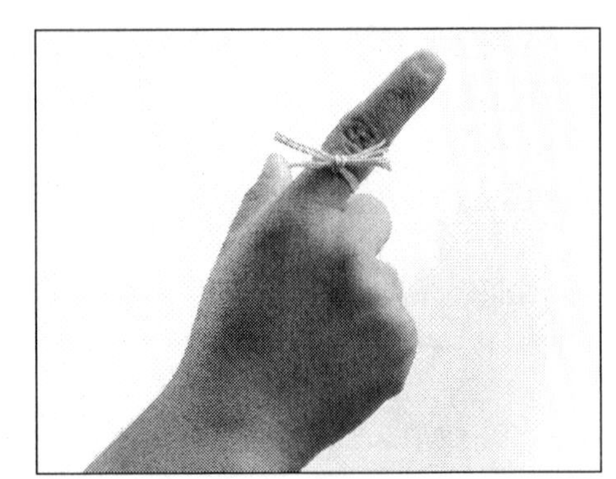

That Reminds Me ...

Share your **thoughts** and **ideas** about your story.

Think about **another story** you have read or heard that is like this one.

Think about things that have happened in **real life**.

Compare your story to another one. Complete the chart.

	In my story	In another story I know
Main character		
Where the story takes place		
When the story takes place		
What happens in my story		

Applying

My name: ______________________

Title of my book: ______________________

Author: ______________________

Ask the Author

Pretend that you meet the author of your story.

Think about **four** things that you want to ask him or her.

Write your **questions** on the lines below.

1. ______________________

____

2. ______________________

____

3. ______________________

____

4. ______________________

____

What is one thing you would like to **tell** the author?

____

____

Applying

My name: ______________________

Title of my book: ______________________

Author: ______________________

A Summer Visitor!

Pretend that the **main character** is coming to stay at your house for the whole summer.

You need to get a **bedroom** ready for her/him.

List 10 things this character will want in the bedroom.

1. ______________________
2. ______________________
3. ______________________
4. ______________________
5. ______________________
6. ______________________
7. ______________________
8. ______________________
9. ______________________
10. ______________________

Draw and **color** a room to show all 10 things in the bedroom.

Applying

My name: ______________________

Title of my book: ______________________

Author: ______________________

How Does It End?

Think about the **beginning** of your story.

Write down the **first thing** that happens.

____

Complete the chart.

The most important event is	**I think this is the most important event because**
The story ended like this	**I knew the story would end this way because**

Analysing

My name: ______________________

Title of my book: ______________________

Author: ______________________

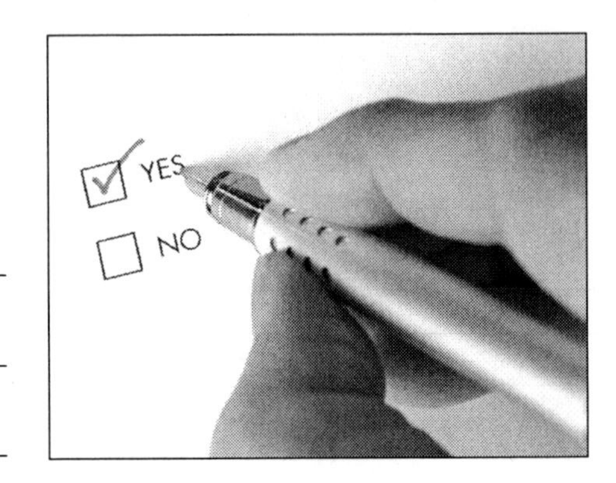

Yes or No

Look in your story for facts that are true.

Now think about some facts that are not true.

Write **4 true facts** and **4 untrue facts** in the chart.

True Facts from my story	Untrue facts about my story
1.	1.
2.	2.
3.	3.
4.	4.

Analysing

My name: ______________________________

Title of my book: ______________________________

Author: ______________________________

My Character is ...

Think about any character in your story.

Complete these sentences.

1. The character I have picked is ______________________________

Tell how he or she **acted**: e.g **brave, helpful, smart**

2. __________ is ______________________________

3. __________ was __________ when ______________________________

____

4. __________ was __________ because ______________________________

____

Draw and **color** a picture to show how your character acted.

My name: ______________________

Title of my book: ______________________

Author: ______________________

Why Did It Happen?

A **cause** is the **reason** something **happens**.

An **effect** is the **thing** that **happens**.

Find **3 important events** in your story.
Write these events in the **Effect** column.

Then write the reason it happened in the **Cause** column.

Effect: the thing that happened	**Cause:** the reason this happened
1.	1.
2.	2.
3.	3.

Analysing

My name: ______________________

Title of my book: ______________________

Author: ______________________

Can You Guess?

Make up **2 riddles** about the **animals, people** or **places** in your story.

Write **3 clues for each riddle**. Write the **answer** at the end.

Riddle #1

1. ______________________
2. ______________________
3. ______________________

I am ______________________

Riddle #2

1. ______________________
2. ______________________
3. ______________________

I am ______________________

My name: ______________________

Title of my book: ______________________

Author: ______________________

Character Friend

Which character from your story would you pick for your friend?

Write the name here ______________________

Now **complete** these sentences. Use the character's **name** in your answers.

1. I would pick ______________________ to be my friend because

____

2. ______________________ and I are the same because

____

3. ______________________ and I are different because

____

Draw and **color** a picture to show you and your new friend having fun.

Analysing

My name: ______________________

Title of my book: ______________________

Author: ______________________

What's the Problem?

Think about one character in the story who had a **problem**.

1. Tell **what problem** he or she had.
2. Tell how he or she **solved** the **problem**.

The **problem** my character had was ______________________

He /she **solved** it ______________________

____

____

____

____

____

____

I think this was a **good solution** because ______________________

____

My name: ______________________________

Title of my book: ______________________________

Author: ______________________________

I liked... I did not like

Think about parts of the story you **liked** and **did not like**.

Complete the chart by telling **3 things you liked** and **3 things you did not like**.

I liked	I did not like
1.	1.
2.	2.
3.	3.

Evaluating

My name: ____________________

Title of my book: ____________________

Author: ____________________

Letter to the Author

Write a letter to the author to tell him or her how you felt about the story.

Complete each sentence in your own words.

(date) ____________________

Dear ____________________

I have just finished reading your story called ____________________.

____________________. I thought it ____________________.

____________________.

I really liked the part ____________________

____________________.

I was wondering about ____________________

____________________.

If you write another story, ____________________

____________________.

Your reading friend,

____

Evaluating

My name: ______________________________

Title of my book: ______________________________

Author: ______________________________

Real or Make Believe?

Is this story **real** or did the author **make it up**?

I think this story is ______________________

Write **4 facts** that **prove** your answer.

1. ____

____

2. ____

____

3. ____

____

4. ____

____

Evaluating

My name: ______________________________

Title of my book: ______________________________

Author: ______________________________

Book of the Year

Pretend that you have been asked to design a trophy for your story.

It will be the **Book of the Year** award.

Draw and **color** the trophy. Think about what to put on your trophy.

1. The words **Book of the Year**.
2. The **title** of the book.
3. The **year**.

My name: ______________________

Title of my book: ______________________

Author: ______________________

Rate a Book

You want to tell others to **read** or **not read** this book.

Use cookies to rate your book.

I did not like it — not bad — good — great — super!

Complete the sentences:

1. This book is ________ real ________ make-believe.
2. It is about ______________________
____
3. The pictures in this story ______________________
____
4. I would tell a friend ______________________

Draw cookies to complete the sentence.

I would give this book ______________________ cookies.

Evaluating

My name: ____________________

Title of my book: ____________________

Author: ____________________

And After This ...

Write what happened at the **end** of your story.

____

____

____

Write what you think might **happen next**. Complete the sentences.

I think the characters will ____________________

____

I think they would do this because ____________________

____

I think a new place they would go is ____________________

because ____________________

My name: ___________________________

Title of my book: ___________________________

Author: ___________________________

Character School Picture

Pretend your character is in your class and you are having your school pictures taken.

Inside the frame, **draw** and **color** a picture of your character.

Complete the sentence under the picture.

This is ___________________ when he /she was in Grade ____ at ___________________________ School.

Creating

My name: ______________________________

Title of my book: ______________________________

Author: ______________________________

Story Puzzle

Pick your **favorite part** of the story.

In the frame, **draw** and **color** a picture to show this part.

Cut your pictures into puzzle pieces.

Give your puzzle to a friend to try.

Title of story: ______________________________

Creating

My name: ____________________

Title of my book: ____________________

Author: ____________________

About the Author

Think about the author of your story.

Then **complete** the following sentences.

The **author** of my book is ____________________

The **kind of stories** he or she writes is ____________________

The **thing I like best** about this author's writing is ____________________

____

Now think about **3 questions** that you would like to ask the author.

Write them on the lines. Remember to use a **?** at the end.

1. ____________________

2. ____________________

3. ____________________

Creating

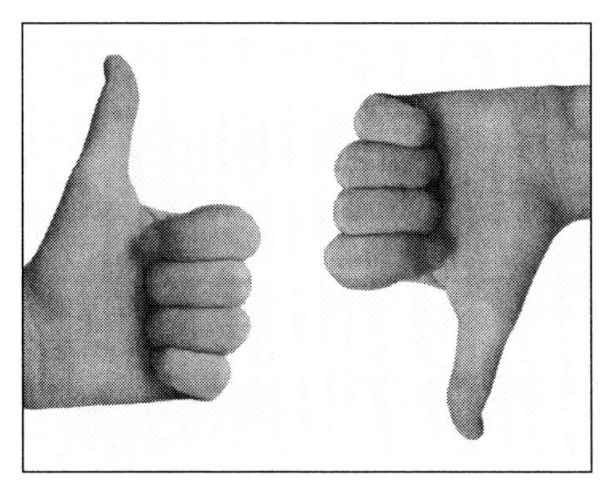

After You Read

My name: ______________________________

Title of my book: ______________________________

Author: ______________________________

Good or Bad?

Think about **one character** in your story.

Tell how you know this character is **good** or **bad**.

Write 4 sentences from your story to **prove** your choice.

My character ____________________ is ______________ because:

1. ______________________________
____

2. ______________________________
____

3. ______________________________
____

4. ______________________________
____

Creating

After You Read

My name: ______________________________

Title of my book: ______________________________

Author: ______________________________

Word Search

Think of good words to describe the **character, setting** and **action** in your story. Write **3 words** for each column in the chart.

Words to find:

Character	Setting	Action

Now **write** these words on the word search frame.

Fill in the other squares with letters.

Give your Word Search to a friend to try!

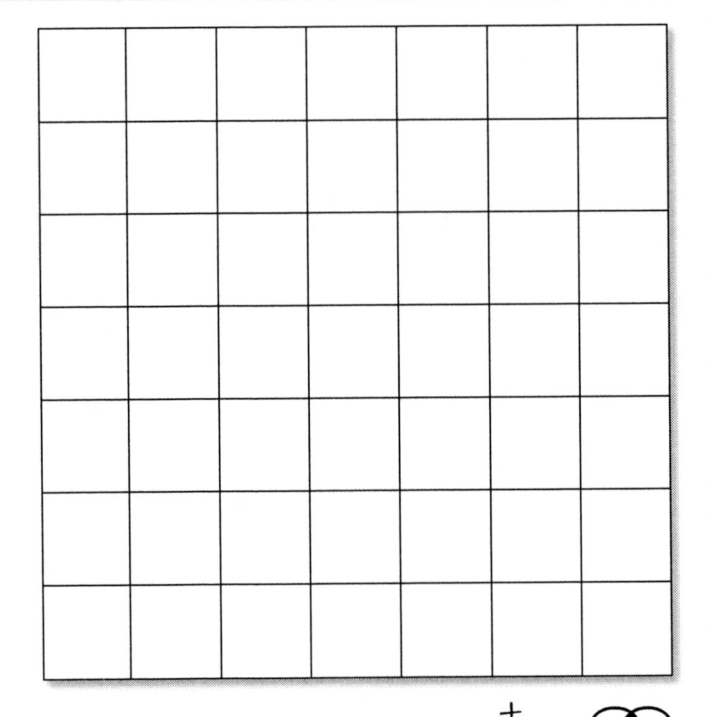

Creating

Language Arts

1. **Retell** the story using flannel board cutout and flannel board.

2. **Scroll Story:** Use a long narrow strip of paper. Draw pictures to retell the story. Write a caption or short sentence for each picture. At one end on the back of the sheet, write the title and the name of the book. Roll up the story and tie with yarn or string.

3. **Accordion Book**: Fold a big rectangular sheet of paper into 4-6 sections. Fold like a fan. On the first page (section), write the title of the book and the author's name.

4. For **non-fiction books:** Make your own "Fact Book", "Did you Know?" book, shape book, "Ask Me!" book (student writes questions and answers)

5. Write a **letter** from the author to the reader. Author will tell the readers a few hints about the story and why they should read the book.

6. Write a **commercial** for the book. Read aloud using (real or toy) microphone.

7. **Character Quiz:** Play similar to 20 questions. The student who is "It" will answer "Yes" or "No" questions and keep the tally. This works best when at least 10 students have finished reading a book and all books are displayed at the time of the game. It helps narrow the choice for very young readers.

MY NAME: ___________________________

Language Arts

8. **Teeny Tiny Books:** Make some small booklets eg. page size 3″x5″ having six to eight pages. Students retell their story in pictures and words. Share with classmates.

9. **Character Clues:** Each child brings three to five items that are related to the story and to the main character. Place items in a paper bag. When presenting, the child gives a clue like "My character uses this to store honey". Keep giving clues until character is guessed.

10. **Sh! Sh! Sh! :** retell the story using a whisper voice.

11. **Try It, You'll Like It! :** Write the title on chart paper. Have students add their book titles to the list.

12. Write an **acrostic poem** using the letters in the name of the main character. Illustrate.

13. **"I'm a Bookworm" game:** First student starts with "I'm a bookworm and I have read (says title of their book)" Second student says "I'm a bookworm and I have read (first title) and (adds own title)" Continue with subsequent students.

14. **Senses Charts:** Set up charts entitled "Sounds, Smells and Sights". Let the students record ideas from their stories under the correct heading.

Visual Arts

1. **Touchable Picture:** Draw and color a picture showing a scene from the story. Use real materials (yarn, cotton balls, fabric, ribbon, wire, leaves, sand)to enhance details.

2. **Life-size main characters:** Trace around the child to make a large figure. Color and add details to depict main character. Cut out figure.

3. **Mural:** A good application for this is when doing an author study. The mural can be divided into sections that will show individual books written by the same author. Two or more students could work on the same section.

4. **Story Book Cube:** Provide students with a flat pattern of a cube. Number the sections. In section #1, write the name of the book and the author. In the subsequent sections, retell the story in pictures and words.

5. **Character Puppets:** Provide students with size appropriate oval shapes to be used to show story character faces. Attach to wooden popsicle sticks. Use to retell story.

6. Make a **birthday card** for the main character in the story. Discuss ideas for messages for inside of card.

7. **Cone Characters:** Provide students with a semicircle pattern. Ask students to draw on facial features, hair, hat, etc. Staple into cone shape.

MY NAME: ______________________

Drama, Dance, Music

1. As a student reads the story aloud, classmates **perform sound effects** (as agreed upon before reading begins).

2. **Introducing** ..... Students read the title, author and a favorite part of the story on to an audio tape. When presenting, play the tape and the student may show the picture that goes with that part.

3. **Dress Up Character Day:** Have a dress-up day for small groups or for the whole class. Classmates try to guess the names of characters.

4. **Silly Songs:** Make up a silly song about characters, plot using a familiar tune. E.g. (tune "Row, Row, Row Your Boat")

   Jack, Jack, Jack was brave. Climbed up to the sky.

   Stole the gold, away he ran. Made that giant cry!

5. Make a **Sing Along Book** using **Silly Songs.**

6. Play appropriate background music while student gives book talk.

7. **Pantomime: List three events in the story.** Act out an event in the story. Ask classmates to guess which one was being shown.

8. Use **rhythm bands instruments** to provide background music.

9. Use **voice** to convey tone and expression while reading dialog from the story.

10. **Make up a chant** to tell about the story.

Crossword Puzzle
Action Words

Word List

cry	play
eat	ride
grow	run
help	sit
hide	sleep
jump	smile

Across

1. We do this with food.
2. Can you .... a pony?
3. We .... when we are hurt.
4. We do this at night.
5. ...... over the rope.
6. Sun and water help plants to ....

Down

1. Will you ..... with me?
2. You will win if you ..... fast.
3. Let's play ..... and seek.
4. Not a frown but a ....
5. Will you ..... me?
6. We do this on a chair.

Hands-On Activities

MY NAME: ______________________________

Word Search
Who Can Be a Character?

Words are placed across and up and down.

bear	boy	dog	fish	hen	pig
bird	dad	duck	girl	mom	wolf

d	o	i	d	a	g	t	n	p	i	g	o
q	b	i	r	d	r	t	d	e	d	i	u
w	e	r	v	o	t	p	b	e	a	r	o
z	x	c	i	g	b	n	o	m	a	l	d
e	m	s	p	d	f	d	y	h	j	r	e
w	o	l	f	v	b	v	b	n	m	n	d
a	m	o	r	d	u	c	k	k	f	d	a
c	l	k	r	a	a	g	y	c	i	b	s
i	q	a	w	d	e	t	x	t	s	y	u
l	t	a	x	d	f	g	r	h	h	e	n

MY NAME: ___________________________

Comprehension Quiz

Mrs. Gray lived in a tiny house just outside our town. She was a kind and happy old lady. But very few people ever went to visit her.

Mrs. Gray didn't mind because she had other visitors. She loved animals. She would feed any strays that came to her door. Sometimes the strays would become her pets. People would laugh at her for helping so many strange animals.

Some people began to wonder how Mrs. Gray could feed so many animals. "How can she do it? She must have a lot of money", they said to themselves.

One night two robbers came to Mrs. Gray's house. It was dark and they crept inside very quietly. They couldn't see where they were going. The first robber fell over a furry lump. The second robber fell right on top of him!

All at once, there was a terrible smell! The robbers screamed "My eyes! My eyes!". Their eyes burned! They raced out of the house and ran down the road. They may be still running!

MY NAME: ________________________

Comprehension Quiz

Answer the questions by **circling** the **correct letter.**

Word Meaning: Choose the meaning used in the story.

1. **strange:** a) not well-known b) odd c) surprising d) old
2. **can:** a) an opener b) a tin c) to be able d) a way of keeping food
3. **burned:** a) to be on fire b) to give off a light c) to hurt badly d) blazed

4. Which sentence is true?
   a) Mrs. Gray was very rich.
   b) A lot of people visited Mrs. Gray
   c) The first robber fell down.
   d) Mrs. Gray had many children.

5. Mrs. Gray is a) lonely b) rich c) kind d) cruel

6. The best title for this story is:
   a) Hidden Money
   b) A Reward for Robbers
   c) Mrs. Gray's Pets
   d) Lost Friends

7. What did the robbers fall over?
   a) a chair b) a dog c) toys d) a skunk

Publication Listing

Ask Your Dealer About Our Complete Line

REMEDIAL EDUCATION

Reading Level 3-4 Grades 5-8

ENVIRONMENTAL STUDIES

ITEM #	TITLE
	MANAGING OUR WASTE SERIES
CC5764	Waste: At the Source
CC5765	Prevention, Recycling & Conservation
CC5766	Waste: The Global View
CC5767	Waste Management Big Book
	CLIMATE CHANGE SERIES #1
CC5769	Global Warming: Causes
CC5770	Global Warming: Effects
CC5771	Global Warming: Reduction
CC5772	Global Warming Big Book
	CLIMATE CHANGE SERIES #2
CC5773	Conservation: Fresh Water Resources
CC5774	Conservation: Ocean Water Resources
CC5775	Conservation: Waterway Habitats Resources
CC5776	Water Conservation Big Book

LANGUAGE ARTS

ITEM #	TITLE
	WRITING SKILLS SERIES
CC1100	How to Write a Paragraph
CC1101	How to Write a Book Report
CC1102	How to Write an Essay
CC1103	Master Writing Big Book

SCIENCE

ITEM #	TITLE
	ECOLOGY & THE ENVIRONMENT SERIES
CC4500	Ecosystems
CC4501	Classification & Adaptation
CC4502	Cells
CC4503	Ecology & The Environment Big Book
	MATTER & ENERGY SERIES
CC4504	Properties of Matter
CC4505	Atoms, Molecules & Elements
CC4506	Energy
CC4507	The Nature of Matter Big Book
	HUMAN BODY SERIES
CC4516	Cells, Skeletal & Muscular Systems
CC4517	Nervous, Senses & Respiratory Systems
CC4518	Circulatory, Digestive Excretory & Reproductive
CC4519	Human Body Big Book
	FORCE & MOTION SERIES
CC4508	Force
CC4509	Motion
CC4510	Simple Machines
CC4511	Force, Motion & Simple Machines Big Book
	SPACE & BEYOND SERIES
CC4512	Space - Solar Systems
CC4513	Space - Galaxies & The Universe
CC4514	Space - Travel & Technology
CC4515	Space Big Book

SOCIAL STUDIES

ITEM #	TITLE
	WORLD CONTINENTS SERIES
CC5750	North America
CC5751	South America
CC5768	The Americas Big Book
CC5752	Europe
CC5753	Africa
CC5754	Asia
CC5755	Australia
CC5756	Antarctica
	NORTH AMERICAN GOVERNMENTS SERIES
CC5757	American Government
CC5758	Canadian Government
CC5759	Mexican Government
CC5760	Governments of North America Big Book
	WORLD GOVERNMENTS SERIES
CC5761	World Political Leaders
CC5762	World Electoral Processes
CC5763	Capitalism versus Communism
CC5777	World Politics Big Book
	WORLD CONFLICT SERIES
CC5500	American Civil War
CC5501	World War I
CC5502	World War II
CC5503	World Wars I & II Big Book
CC5505	Korean War
CC5506	Vietnam War
CC5507	Korean & Vietnam Wars Big Book
CC5508	Persian Gulf War (1990-1991)
CC5509	Iraq War (2003-Present)
CC5510	Gulf Wars Big Book

VISIT:
www.CLASSROOM COMPLETE PRESS.com
To view sample pages from each book

Publication Listing

Ask Your Dealer About Our Complete Line

REGULAR EDUCATION

LANGUAGE ARTS

ITEM #	TITLE
	LITERACY SKILL SERIES #1
CC1106	Reading Response Forms: Grades 1-2
CC1107	Reading Response Forms: Grades 3-4
CC1108	Reading Response Forms: Grades 5-6
CC1109	Reading Response Forms Big Book
	LITERACY SKILL SERIES #2
CC1110	Word Families - Short Vowels: Grades K-1
CC1111	Word Families - Long Vowels: Grades K-1
CC1112	Word Families Big Book: Grades K-1
	LITERACY SKILL SERIES #3
CC1113	High Frequency Sight Words: Grades K-1
CC1114	High Frequency Picture Words: Grades K-1
CC1115	Sight & Picture Words Big Book Grades K-1

LITERATURE KITS™

ITEM #	TITLE
	GRADES 1-2
CC2100	Curious George (H. A. Rey)
CC2101	Paper Bag Princess (Robert N. Munsch)
CC2102	Stone Soup (Marcia Brown)
CC2103	The Very Hungry Caterpillar (Eric Carle)
CC2104	Where the Wild Things Are (Maurice Sendak)
	GRADES 3-4
CC2300	Babe: The Gallant Pig (Dick King-Smith)
CC2301	Because of Winn-Dixie (Kate DiCamillo)
CC2302	The Tale of Despereaux (Kate DiCamillo)
CC2303	James and the Giant Peach (Roald Dahl)
CC2304	Ramona Quimby, Age 8 (Beverly Cleary)
CC2305	The Mouse and the Motorcycle (Beverly Cleary)
CC2306	Charlotte's Web (E.B. White)
CC2307	Owls in the Family (Farley Mowat)
CC2308	Sarah, Plain and Tall (Patricia MacLachlan)
CC2309	Matilda (Roald Dahl)
CC2310	Charlie & The Chocolate Factory (Roald Dahl)

LITERATURE KITS™

ITEM #	TITLE
	GRADES 5-6
CC2500	Black Beauty (Anna Sewell)
CC2501	Bridge to Terabithia (Katherine Paterson)
CC2502	Bud, Not Buddy (Christopher Paul Curtis)
CC2503	The Egypt Game (Zilpha Keatley Snyder)
CC2504	The Great Gilly Hopkins (Katherine Paterson)
CC2505	Holes (Louis Sachar)
CC2506	Number the Stars (Lois Lowry)
CC2507	The Sign of the Beaver (E.G. Speare)
CC2508	The Whipping Boy (Sid Fleischman)
CC2509	Island of the Blue Dolphins (Scott O'Dell)
CC2510	Underground to Canada (Barbara Smucker)
CC2511	Loser (Jerry Spinelli)
CC2512	The Higher Power of Lucky (Susan Patron)
CC2513	Kira-Kira (Cynthia Kadohata)
CC2514	Dear Mr. Henshaw (Beverly Cleary)
CC2515	The Summer of the Swans (Betsy Byars)
	GRADES 7-8
CC2700	Cheaper by the Dozen (Frank B. Gilbreth)
CC2701	The Miracle Worker (William Gibson)
CC2702	The Red Pony (John Steinbeck)
CC2703	Treasure Island (Robert Louis Stevenson)
CC2704	Romeo and Juliet (William Shakespeare)

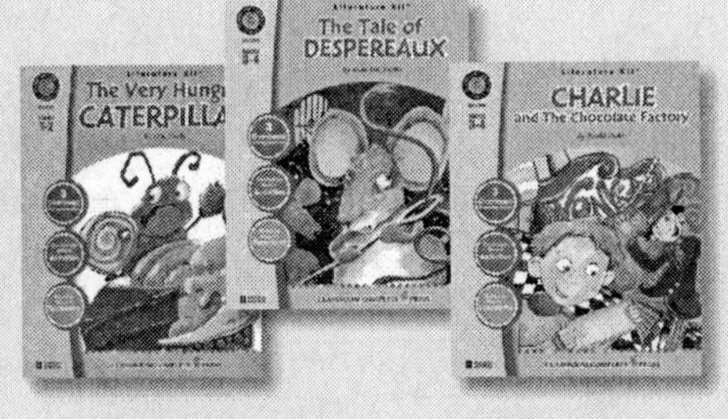